line drawings for many fiction titles.
He lives in Wales.

For a complete list of
Horrid Henry titles, visit

www.horridhenry.co.uk

or

www.orionbooks.co.uk

A HORRID FACTBOOK

HORRID HENRY'S
SPACE

Francesca Simon
Illustrated by Tony Ross

Orion
Children's Books

First published in Great Britain in 2014
by Orion Children's Books
a division of the Orion Publishing Group Ltd
Orion House
5 Upper Saint Martin's Lane
London WC2H 9EA
An Hachette UK company

1 3 5 7 9 10 8 6 4 2

Text © Francesca Simon 2014
Illustrations © Tony Ross 2014

Facts compiled by Sally Byford.

ISBN 978 1 4440 1446 4

A catalogue record for this book is available from the British Library.

Printed in Great Britain by
Clays Ltd, St Ives plc

www.orionbooks.co.uk

www.horridhenry.co.uk

CONTENTS

This book contains a very special
illustration by artist Ben Matthews,
aged 10. Ben was diagnosed with a disease
called Burkitt's lymphoma in April 2013.
Ben has always dreamed of becoming
an illustrator, and this year the Starlight
Foundation was able to grant his wish to
meet *Horrid Henry* illustrator, Tony Ross.

Ben spent the day with Tony at his house
in Wales, where Ben helped Tony with one
of the illustrations in this factbook. Turn to
page 53 to see Ben's Martian landscape.

Hello from Henry

Hey gang!

Space. The final frontier . . . as some clever-clogs philosopher once said, i.e. ME.

Space is so . . . spacey. It's full of planets and meteors and stars and asteroids waiting to be named after me, and little green men made of cheese — or was that goats? But best of all, find out how to wee in space!

Happy flying,

Henry

WHAT'S OUT THERE?

Space starts around **100 km** above Earth, beyond the blue sky and clouds.

It's called 'space' because it looks like there's just big **empty space** between all the stars and planets – but space is definitely **not** empty.

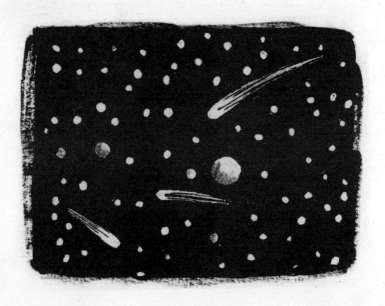

Scientists believe there are around **500 billion galaxies** in space. Each galaxy is made up of stars, planets, gases and dust.

Planet Earth lies within a galaxy called the **Milky Way**, which is shaped like a huge **whirlpool** and contains about 200–400 billion stars.

Our **Sun** is **just one** of the stars in the Milky Way.

Around the Sun there are eight planets, five **dwarf planets** and over **100 moons**. They make up what we call the **Solar System**.

There used to be nine planets, but in 2006, scientists decided **Pluto** wasn't big enough to be called a planet. It's now known as a **dwarf planet**.

An **asteroid** is a rock found in the Asteroid Belt between Mars and Jupiter. Some asteroids are as **big as houses**, while others are as **small as a grain of sand**.

Sometimes asteroids fall towards Earth – and when they do this they are called **meteorites**. Usually they **explode** in the sky before they reach Earth, but occasionally they **crash** into our planet, shaking the ground like an **earthquake** and creating deep **craters**.

The most famous asteroid was the one that hit Earth **65 million years** ago. It caused such dramatic changes to the weather that many scientists believe this is the reason why the **dinosaurs** died out.

On the very edge of the Solar System, millions of **comets** are speeding around in every direction. Comets are balls of dust and ice which look like **dirty snowballs**. When they travel close to the Sun, they start to melt and grow **long tails** – you can sometimes see the brightest ones trailing across the sky.

The **Universe** is the term for **everything** that scientists know exists, including **planets**, **stars** and **suns**. The Universe is so huge that no one really knows how big it is. The more scientists explore, the more they find!

Most scientists believe that the Universe began around 14 billion years ago with the **Big Bang**. They say it started with a tiny bubble, **smaller than a pinhead**, which got so hot it suddenly **exploded** out into the huge Universe we know today.

I wonder if that Big Bang was as loud as one of Moody Margaret's shrieks?

Some scientists think the Universe will **keep on growing**. Others believe that one day, billions of years in the future, all the galaxies will **shrink** towards each other and – CRASH! – end in a **Big Crunch**.

LIFT OFF!

There are organisations all over the world, including **NASA** (the National Aeronautics and Space Administration) in the USA and the **Space Agency** in the UK, which plan space travel, train astronauts and design spacecraft.

Spacecraft are all the different types of **machines** designed to travel in space.

Rockets are fast and powerful spacecraft designed to break through Earth's gravity and zoom into space at speeds of **40,000 km per hour**.

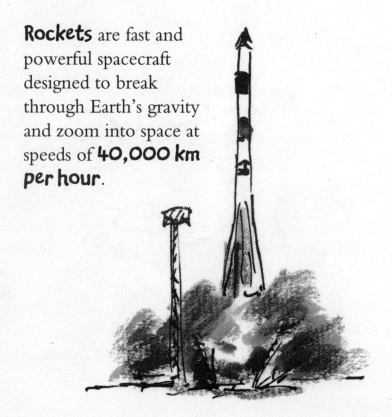

Lunar modules are spacecraft that astronauts use to land on the **Moon**.

Moon buggies are spacecraft that astronauts drive once they're on the Moon. It's a **bumpy ride** over the rocks and craters, but moon buggies are built to be tough.

Command modules are spacecraft that return astronauts from the Moon back to Earth.

Some spacecraft **orbit** the Moon, the Earth or another planet, meaning they **travel in a path around it**.

Space stations are spacecraft that **stay in orbit** around the Earth. Astronauts can live in them for **months**, doing experiments and making discoveries.

Just think if I could be in one – no Peter, no Miss Battle-Axe. How do I apply??!

The biggest-ever **space station** is the **ISS** (International Space Station). It was built piece by piece in space – the first part was launched in **1998** and the final part in **2011** – and it's now **the size of a football field**.

Space shuttles transport astronauts up to the space stations and back to Earth again. These spacecraft can be used many times – they land on Earth by gliding along a runway, **like an aeroplane**.

Orbiters are smaller spacecraft designed to go into orbit. They take astronauts around the Earth and the Moon.

Some types of spacecraft operate without anyone inside. These are called **robotic spacecraft**. Robotic spacecraft have visited all the planets in our Solar System – and have even **landed** on Venus and Mars.

Robotic orbiters orbit slowly around planets, taking photographs. This helps us to make **maps** of other planets.

Satellites are robotic spacecraft which orbit Earth. They can be used to find out things like what the weather is going to be several days in the future. They send information back to Earth via radio signals.

Landers are robotic spacecraft which land on planets. They collect samples of soil and rock by using their robotic arms and rock-grinding tools, and send the information back to Earth.

Space probes travel so fast that they can venture further into space than any other spacecraft – past the planets and even out past the Solar System itself.

Voyager 1 and **Voyager 2** are **space probes**. They have already been travelling for over **35 years**. Voyager 1 has travelled the furthest, reaching right to the edge of our Solar System.

LIFE IN SPACE

Gravity is what keeps us firmly on the ground on Earth. In space there is hardly any gravity, so astronauts **float** about like **balloons**. They can even do **somersaults** in the air!

Ever had that **sinking feeling** in your stomach on a roller coaster or a lift as it starts to go down? That's how space travellers feel for the first few days – it can make them **very sick**!

Some astronauts just take a quick trip to space to visit the Moon, but many **live and work** in space stations, spending weeks or even **months** there.

It's so easy to move about in space that astronauts have to do lots of **exercise** – more than two hours a day if they are away for six months – to stop their muscles **wasting away**. Otherwise they can't walk properly when they get home.

The first foods invented for astronauts were **dried powders** and tasteless **pastes**, but scientists soon developed **new and tasty** space food. Now there are proper meals like chicken stew, scrambled eggs and even **chocolate pudding**.

What? No burgers? No crisps? No pizza? Cancel my trip!

There's no room for a **fridge** on board most spacecraft, so food is **frozen** and **dried** in pouches or cans, and water is only added when the crew are ready to eat.

Being in space reduces astronauts' **senses** of smell and taste, so all the food has to be **extra spicy** so they can actually **taste** and enjoy it.

Astronauts eat out of plastic bowls. These are attached to a tray by **fabric fasteners**, and the tray is attached to a table or to the astronaut – otherwise their lunch would **float away**!

Messy eaters are banned in space! Stray crumbs float around and drops of liquid form floating **globules** which could cause damage to the crew or the spaceship.

Astronauts can't pop to the supermarket when they run out of food. If they are staying in space for a long time, **rockets** are sent on special missions to deliver supplies.

Ever wondered how astronauts go to the **toilet**? They have to wear seatbelts so they don't float away, and instead of flushing, everything gets **sucked away** into special containers.

Astronauts have to practise on a training toilet with a video camera under the rim, watching their own **bottom** on a screen to check that they know how to sit properly. If you get it wrong in space, your poo could go floating off around the spacecraft!

You can't open the windows on a spacecraft, so **farting** is definitely a no-no. Certain foods, like **beans** and **cabbage**, are banned as a result.

YES!

There isn't a lot of water in space, so astronauts have to **wash** themselves with damp towels and clean their hair with special rinse-free shampoo.

Time for bed! At night, astronauts are strapped down in **sleeping bags** to stop them floating around the spacecraft.

If astronauts venture out of their spacecraft, they need to wear space suits to protect them from the **extreme temperatures**. Space can be as **cold** as **minus 120°C** or as **hot** as **120°C**.

The average space suit weighs about **122 kg**. It takes an astronaut around **45 minutes** to get into it.

Space suits contain special **high-tech** shorts that hold up to **two litres** of liquid – so astronauts don't need to worry about returning to the spaceship for the toilet. They can just **go in their suits**!

It's easy for astronauts to keep in touch with Earth. They can send **emails**, chat on the phone and even **see** their families via video links.

FANTASTIC
FIRSTS

First spacecraft in space: The Russian Sputnik 1, a robotic orbiter, launched on 4 October **1957**. Sputnik 1 was only the size of a football, but it changed history forever.

First moon landing: the **Russian** space probe Luna 2 took 36 hours to travel into space. It **crashed** on the surface of the Moon in **1959**.

First living creature in space: Laika, a stray dog, orbited Earth in the Russian Sputnik 2, which launched only a month later than Sputnik 1, in November **1957**.

First man in space: Russian Yuri Gagarin made one orbit of Earth in the first ever manned orbiter spacecraft, Vostok 1, in **1961**.

First woman in space: Valentina Tereshkova, also from Russia, was the pilot of Vostok 6. She orbited Earth for three days in **1963**.

First spacewalk: In March **1965**, Alexey Leonov left Russia's Voskhod 2 for 12 minutes to carry out repairs on the spacecraft.

First men on the moon: Apollo 11 astronauts, Neil Armstrong and Buzz Aldrin, stepped onto the moon's surface and planted the American flag on 20 July **1969**. They were watched on TV by **600 million** people.

First space station: In April **1971**, the Russian Salyut 1 space station was launched. The three astronauts on it spent three weeks orbiting Earth.

Can you imagine if they'd been me, Rude Ralph and Greedy Graham?

First moon buggy: In July **1971**, Apollo 15 astronauts spent around three hours driving a buggy on the moon, exploring its hills and valleys.

First spiderweb in space: In **1973**, two **spiders** called Arabella and Anita went into orbit in the Skylab 3 space station, as an experiment to see if spiders could spin webs in space. Arabella was the first to spin a web.

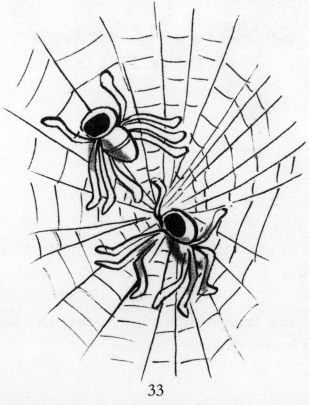

First British astronaut in space: Helen Sharman was selected from over 13,000 applicants to represent the UK on the Russian space mission, Project Juno, in **1989**. She took a **photograph of the Queen** with her.

First space tourist: American Dennis Tito paid **£20 million** for an eight-day holiday on board a Russian mission to the International Space Station in **2001**.

I'd pay - just let me check Peter's piggybank and I'll get back to you.

SUPER SUN

The **Sun** is the star at the **centre** of our Solar System – and all the planets **orbit** around it.

Like me, really.

The Sun is the only star that's close enough to Earth for us to feel its heat – but it's actually a whopping **150 million km** away!

Like all stars, the Sun is a huge ball of
super-hot gas – 6,000°C on the outside
– more than 20 times hotter than an oven
on maximum heat – and an amazing
15 million°C in the centre.

Stars don't live forever, but scientists think
that the Sun has enough fuel to last for at least
another **5 billion years** before it starts to die.

The Sun might look smooth and round, but close up it's as **rough as a stormy sea**. It shoots out towering pillars of flames and violent **explosions** of hot gas.

Just one square cm of the Sun's surface shines as brightly as more than **230,000 candles**.

No one has ever been very close to the Sun.
From 5 million km away, it's so hot that it
could kill a space-walking astronaut, and
from **2 million km** away it could **melt a
spacecraft like an ice lolly**.

The Sun measures **1.4 million km** across –
that's 300,000 times bigger than Earth. If the
Sun was the size of a **football**, Earth would
be around the size of a **pea** in comparison.

A couple of times a year, there is a **solar eclipse**. This is when the Moon travels in front of the Earth and **hides** some of the Sun from view. If you're in the right part of the world at the right time, you might actually see it happen.

A total eclipse is when the Moon completely hides the Sun and the sky goes dark – even during the day. This only happens once every 18 months, and it only happens in the same place **once every 400 years**. The last one was in in Africa in November 2013, and the next one will be in Europe in March 2015 – so **watch out** for it!

The Sun doesn't really rise and set — it stays in the same position all the time. It's the Earth which **rotates**, making one complete turn every 24 hours. During this time, different parts of the Earth pass into the Sun's light and then leave it again.

It takes eight minutes for the light from the Sun to reach Earth. So when you watch a **sunset**, it actually happened **eight minutes before**!

If the Sun could be **heard** through the vacuum of space, scientists think it would sound like the loud *ringing of cathedral bells*.

MEGA MOON

The **Moon** is the **only other place** in the Universe where humans have ever set foot.

Our moon is basically a **large ball of rock** – dry, dusty and lifeless, with no air to breathe or water to drink.

Without water or wind, the Moon's surface has stayed unchanged for 3 or 4 billion years. This means that the **footprints** and tyre tracks left behind by astronauts will stay there **forever**.

The Moon does have **mountains**, though – its tallest is **Mons Huygens**, which at 4,700 m high is over half as tall as the highest mountain on Earth, Mount Everest (8,848 m).

When **Neil Armstrong**, the first man on the Moon, stepped out of his spacecraft, his words went down in history: "That's one small step for a man, one **giant leap** for mankind."

It's a steamy **107°C** on the Moon during the day, but a chilly **minus 153°C** at night. Astronauts have to wear space suits to stop their **blood** from either **boiling** or **freezing**.

The Moon is **384,000 km** away from Earth. It takes a spaceship just two days to reach it, but if you could **fly** there in an aeroplane, it would take 26 days.

Earth has much **stronger gravity** than the Moon, which is why the Moon travels around it. It takes around **29½ days** for a complete orbit, and that's how we measure our **months**.

During one orbit of Earth, the Moon goes from being a new moon, when it looks like a thin **crescent**, to a **round** full moon and then back to a crescent again.

Did you know that **moonlight** doesn't actually exist? The Moon has no light of its own – it only looks as if it is shining because light from the Sun **reflects** off its surface.

Earth isn't the only planet with a moon. All the other planets, except Mercury and Venus, have at least one moon of their own – Jupiter has **63**!

PLANET POWER

The four planets closest to the Sun are
Mercury, **Venus**, **Earth** and **Mars**. They are
the **smallest** planets, with **rocky** surfaces.

The four outer planets – **Jupiter**, **Saturn**,
Uranus and **Neptune** – are the biggest. They
are giant balls of **gas**.

Hmmm. Just like Margaret.

It sounds strange, but to understand how
different the sizes of the planets are, it helps
to imagine them as **fruit**. If **Jupiter**
– the biggest planet – was the size of a
watermelon,
Saturn would
be the size of
a **grapefruit**,
Uranus an **apple**,
Neptune an
orange, **Venus** and
Earth two **cherry tomatoes**,
Mars a **blueberry** and **Mercury**
as small as a **pomegranate pip**!

Mercury is the **closest** planet to the Sun –
but it's still **56 million km** away. If you could
drive there in a car, it would take you **57
years!**

Mercury can reach temperatures of up to
427°C during the day – hot enough to melt
lead! At night it drops to well below freezing,
around **minus 600°C**.

Neptune is the **furthest** planet from the sun
– 4.3 billion km away. And if you drove that
distance, it would take you **4,400 years**.

With its bright yellow clouds, **Venus** looks beautiful from space, but it's the most **poisonous** planet in the Solar System – and its clouds of gas keep the Sun's heat in, like a blanket, making it even hotter than Mercury.

Earth is sometimes called the **'Goldilocks'** planet. Like the third bowl of porridge in the fairy tale, it's not too hot and not too cold – and it has **just the right amount** of light and water to **keep us alive.**

Mars has been nicknamed the **Red Planet** because the rocks on its surface are full of **rusty red iron**. The ground is covered with dusty red soil, which gets swept up by the wind and makes pink clouds.

Is there life on **Mars**? Many people think so. In 2014, scientists discovered evidence of an ancient **lake**. This suggests there may have been some sort of **living creatures** on the planet . . . **billions** of years ago.

Mars boasts the largest **volcano** of all the planets – **Olympus Mons**. It is 25 km high – three times higher than Mount Everest.

Jupiter looks as though it's covered in beautiful patterns of cream, brown and blue – they're actually swirling **clouds of gas**, blown about by **powerful wind storms**, which can reach up to **540 km per hour**.

Saturn is best known for the **rings** that spin around it. These rings appear solid, but they are actually **blizzards of ice and rocks** – some chunks as small as grains of sand and others as **big as buses**.

The coldest planet of all, bluey-green **Uranus**, rotates **on its side**. Scientists think this might be because of a **collision** with a large object billions of years ago.

Neptune is a **dark, cold and windy** planet – a big blue ball of poisonous gas that becomes hot liquid below its clouds.

STARS
IN SPACE

Can you believe it? There are more stars in the Universe than all the **grains of sand** on Earth.

Stars are balls of **hot gas** – the hottest stars glow blue-white, the coolest ones are an orange-red colour, and yellow stars like the Sun are in between.

There are around **1,000 billion stars** in the Milky Way alone – that's nearly 200 stars for every person living on Earth today.

Stars look pointy and **twinkly** from Earth, but close up they are shaped more like balls, and they **shine steadily**. It's the air around Earth which makes stars' light twist and bend so they appear to be twinkling.

The brightest star in the night sky apart from the Sun is Sirius — also known as the **Dog Star**. It's about twice as big as the Sun, and it gives out more than 20 times as much light.

Did you know that a **shooting star** isn't a star at all? It's actually a meteroid, a piece of rubbish from the Solar System, **burning up** with a bright streak of light as it hits the Earth's atmosphere.

Stars don't last forever. Smaller stars cool down and end quietly, but big stars go out with a **bang**.

Sometimes the Milky Way is lit up by a huge flash of light as a giant star blows itself apart in a huge, violent explosion, known as a **supernova**.

Supernovas can last for a week or longer, and they shine as brightly as a **galaxy of 100 billion** ordinary stars before finally fading away.

BIGGEST, FASTEST, BRIGHTEST...

Biggest Planet: Giant **Jupiter** is by far the **biggest** planet, measuring 143,884 km across. It's so huge that all the other planets could fit inside it.

Fastest Planet: Mercury speeds around the Sun once every 88 days, at an average speed of **50 km per second**.

Brightest Planet: Venus is so bright it can be seen from Earth without using a telescope. It has been nicknamed both the **Evening Star** and the **Morning Star**.

Most Expensive Space Station: The International Space Station is not only the most expensive space station, it's also the **most expensive object ever made by humans**, costing around **£85 billion** to build and operate.

Instead of building that Space Station, they should have just given all that loot to me.

Most Expensive Holiday: American billionaire Charles Simonyi paid **£35 million** for a 14 day trip into space, taking the Russian Soyuz rocket to the International Space Station in 2009.

Place Most Visited by Humans: 12 people have walked on the **Moon**. In fact, this is the only place in space to have been visited by humans.

Hottest Planet: Venus has a temperature of over **460°C**, and is covered in **erupting volcanoes**.

Coldest Planet: Uranus is a chilly **minus 213°C**.

Smallest Planet: Mercury is so **small** that 18 of it would fit inside the Earth.

Lightest Planet: If it could be put into a giant bath, **Saturn** would be light enough to **float**.

Wettest Planet: The **Earth**, with 71% of its surface covered in water.

Furthest Spacecraft Journey: Space probe **Voyager I** launched in 1977 and is **still going**. It is around 18.7 billion km from the Sun, well beyond the furthest planet, Neptune.

Shortest Day: Jupiter's day lasts nine hours 55 minutes, compared to 24 hours on Earth.

Oldest Person to Travel into Space: John Glenn from the USA was **77 years old** when he went on board the Discovery spacecraft in 1998.

Furthest Human Journey: To the far side of the Moon – over 400 km – on the **Apollo 13** mission in 1970.

Longest Time Spent on the Moon: 74 hours 59 minutes, during the **Apollo 17** mission, launched in December 1972.

Fastest Winds in the Solar System: On **Neptune**, the winds are ten times stronger than a hurricane on Earth.

ARE WE ALONE?

Explorers haven't ever discovered another **living creature** in space, but many people believe **aliens do exist** – and claim that sightings of **UFOs** (Unidentified Flying Objects) prove it.

The most famous UFO sighting was at **Roswell**, USA, in **1947**. According to witnesses, soldiers were seen **removing alien bodies** from what looked like a **crashed spaceship**. The US Air Force denied it was a UFO – they said it was a weather balloon; then later that it was a top-secret military experiment using human-like dummies. Lots of people believe this is just a story to **hide the truth**.

In 1977, 15 children in Wales told their teacher they saw a **silver man** with **pointed ears** get out of a metal spacecraft in a field next to their school. No one believed them, so the children were asked to draw what they had seen – and all their drawings **looked the same**. Were they telling the truth? No one has ever found out . . .

Driving home in **1961** in the **USA**, Betty and Barney Hill saw a **bright light** in the **sky** and left their car to look. They claim they suddenly found themselves **56 km** away, three hours later, with their clothes torn and dirty. They **couldn't remember a thing**, but were convinced they had been **abducted** by aliens.

Two teenagers working at an **American** summer camp in **1969** claimed they were taken on board an alien spacecraft. They said the aliens had slits for noses and **webbed fingers**, but **no ears or lips**. Other people at the camp said that the same thing had also happened to them.

Maybe they just met Peter.

In **1978**, an **American** scientist who was writing about UFOs claimed that a **strange-looking man** came to his door. The man was completely **bald** and had **no lips** – though he was wearing red lipstick to make it look as though he had. He ordered the scientist to destroy all his paperwork on the UFO case – then vanished.

Some people believe that **crop circles** – elaborate patterns created in fields of crops which appear overnight *as if by magic* – are the work of aliens and more evidence they exist. But could they just be people playing tricks?

Lots of UFO and alien stories have **never been explained** – but many others turn out to be **fakes or jokes**.

Traffic stopped and the police were called when **glowing lights** appeared in the skies above Utah, **USA**, in **2011**. Luckily the lights turned out to be **Chinese lanterns** launched by school kids.

Another funny alien sighting was reported by four teenagers in **Panama** in **2009**. They said they were chased by an alien with a small head and skinny arms. One of them had taken a photograph of the alien – which was later identified as a **sloth**.

In **Russia, 2013**, two students claimed they had photographed the body of an alien **frozen** in snow in Russia. They later admitted it was a **fake:** they'd made the alien out of **stale bread** covered in **chicken skin**.

On 4 September **1967**, six shiny flying saucers were found around **Britain**. There was widespread panic, until a group of students admitted it was all a **big joke**. They had made the UFOs out of plastic, filled them with boiled-up bread dough, and attached electronic speakers that made a wailing noise. Then they sneaked out at night and left the UFOs on the ground – ready to be found the following morning.

There are at least two aliens at MY school — Margaret and Miss Battle-Axe — when will scientists come collect them?

So . . . are we alone or not? We don't know – yet. But the two Voyager space probes travelling through outer space are **ready to meet aliens**. They both carry a golden disk on board, with pictures and music from all over the world and people saying **hello** in **55 different languages**.

STRANGE
BUT TRUE

Wish you were a bit **taller**? Try spending a few months in space. Astronauts can grow up to **five cm taller** – without the pull of gravity, their spines relax and **expand**, then **shrink** back again when they return Earth.

It isn't possible to **cry** properly in space – there **isn't enough gravity,** so the tears can't roll down your cheeks.

In **2013** a new planet was discovered – a gas giant 11 times the size of Jupiter. 100,000 *Doctor Who* fans signed a petition to name it 'Gallifrey', the home planet of the time-travelling alien doctor, to celebrate the TV show's 50th birthday. The International Astronomical Union in charge of the naming refused.

In **1991**, the space shuttle Columbia launched with **2,478 jellyfish** on board, to investigate how weightlessness would affect them. It was discovered that the jellyfish couldn't swim as gracefully in space – they had trouble telling up from down!

There are **over 100,000** pieces of man-made **rubbish** floating around in the Solar System. Even the tiniest piece can travel with such speed that it can damage a spacecraft: a **speck of paint** made a hole almost one cm wide in a spacecraft window!

In **1965**, astronaut Edward White lost a **glove** during a spacewalk. It stayed in orbit for a **month** and reached speeds of 28,000 km per hour . . . before falling back to Earth and burning up in the air.

Between 6% and 20% of Americans believe the photos of Apollo 11 landing on the moon on 20 July 1969 were **faked**, and that humans have **never landed on the moon**.

Early spacesuits weren't perfect! When Alexey Leonov made his historic first spacewalk in **1965**, his suit **expanded** so much that he could **barely fit** back through the spacecraft hatch.

If you **discover** a new **asteroid** through your telescope, **you can name it** after your favourite celebrity, writer or fictional character. There's already Asteroid 6223 **Dahl** (named after Roald Dahl), 9007 **James Bond** and 17059 **Elvis**.

Get looking, Purple Hand Gang! The Henry Asteroid is waiting to be discovered.

Moon rocks don't look very special, yet over 100 small ones brought back by the Apollo missions have been **stolen**, and people have been caught trying to sell them.

A **black hole** is what happens when a giant star collapses. It turns into a small dark place with such a strong force of gravity that light can't escape. If a human fell into a black hole, the strength of gravity would stretch them out thinner and thinner, like spaghetti.

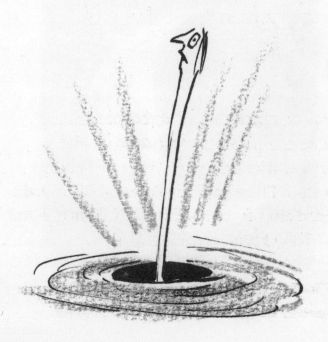

When you look at the **furthest visible star** in the sky, you are actually looking billions of years **back in time**. That's how long it has taken the light from the star to reach you.

On 1 April **2002**, NASA confirmed that the Moon really is made of **green cheese** after finding a 'sell by' date printed on it. It was, of course, a **trick** for **April Fools' Day**!

Bye!

HORRID HENRY BOOKS

Horrid Henry
Horrid Henry and the Secret Club
Horrid Henry Tricks the Tooth Fairy
Horrid Henry's Nits
Horrid Henry Gets Rich Quick
Horrid Henry's Haunted House
Horrid Henry and the Mummy's Curse
Horrid Henry's Revenge
Horrid Henry and the Bogey Babysitter
Horrid Henry's Stinkbomb
Horrid Henry's Underpants
Horrid Henry Meets the Queen
Horrid Henry and the Mega-Mean Time Machine
Horrid Henry and the Football Fiend
Horrid Henry's Christmas Cracker
Horrid Henry and the Abominable Snowman
Horrid Henry Robs the Bank
Horrid Henry Wakes the Dead
Horrid Henry Rocks
Horrid Henry and the Zombie Vampire
Horrid Henry's Monster Movie
Horrid Henry's Nightmare
Horrid Henry's Krazy Ketchup

Early Readers
Don't Be Horrid, Henry!
Horrid Henry's Birthday Party
Horrid Henry's Holiday
Horrid Henry's Underpants
Horrid Henry Gets Rich Quick
Horrid Henry and the Football Fiend
Horrid Henry's Nits
Horrid Henry and Moody Margaret
Horrid Henry's Thank You Letter
Horrid Henry Reads a Book
Horrid Henry's Car Journey
Moody Margaret's School
Horrid Henry Tricks and Treats
Horrid Henry's Christmas Play

Visit Horrid Henry's website at **www.horridhenry.co.uk**
for competitions, games, downloads and a monthly newsletter.

the

orion star